THOUGH HE SLAY ME...

God's Eternal Purposes

Patricia M. Tuckett

Eagles Word Christian Publisher, LLC
New York

Copyright © August 2022 by Patricia M. Tuckett
All rights reserved.
ISBN: 978-1-7374692-4-7

No part of this publication may be reproduced, stored in a retrieval system, or transmitted in any form or by any means, for example, electronic, photocopying, recording without prior written permission of the author. The only exception to this is brief quotations in printed reviews.

Unless otherwise indicated, all Scriptures quotations are taken from the King James Version of the Holy Bible

Printed in the United States of America

God's Eternal Purposes

Dedication

This book is dedicated to the Body of Christ
and to my parents, Eris and Reginald Small
who gave me a Godly foundation

To God Be the Glory!

TABLE OF CONTENTS

Another Day 1
Who Is Job? 2
What's Going On? 4
Questions Without Answers 5
Can You Hear Me? 7
Friends 9
What Happened? 11
What Actually Happened 13
The Process 17
The Process Continued 18
You Have No Power Over Me 19
Faith Is The Victory 21
The Battle Rages 23
The Living Word 25
The Devil's Native Language 27
Freedom 29
Wisdom 31
Increased Knowledge 33
Renewal 36
Divine Set-Up 39
Another Plan 45

The Same Strategy 48
Guaranteed Victory 50
The Mystery Revealed 52
Counted Trustworthy 59
Modern Jobs 62
Getting To Know Him 66
The Ultimate Revelation 69
Life Of Abundance 74
All Because Of Love 82
How To Tap In 87
Don't Be Fooled 90
Spread The Word 93
What's Your Excuse? 97

ACKNOWLEDGMENTS

All thanks and praise to my gracious heavenly Father God who has given me life and breath; to the Lord Jesus Christ who has chosen and ordained me for such a time as this; to Holy Spirit, my Helper, Teacher, and Guide who inspired me to write this book and coached me in the delivery of it.

To my husband, Earl Tuckett, whom God used as the catalyst for the writing of this book.

To my sister Christine Cornwall who graciously read the manuscript, encouraged and supported me in this endeavor.

To my Calvary Cathedral of Praise church family whose love and prayers availed much in the successful completion of this book.

To my editor and publisher, Judy Howard, who was sent by God at the appointed time to assist in making this dream a reality.

PREFACE

This book was borne out of a burning desire to share deep spiritual truths that have greatly enriched my life.

There is nothing superficial about God, and there are deep spiritual truths that He wants to reveal to each of us.

These truths come by divine revelation according to our capacity to receive (the Spirit revealing the Word). Once we have received, it is ours to keep, not just for our own consumption, but to share with others so that their lives too can be enriched.

We're on this exciting journey of life together. We are here to love, enjoy, and enrich each other, all for the glory of God.

May you be blessed and your life greatly enriched as you read.

INTRODUCTION

Why do bad things happen to good people? Why do the wicked prosper? Why is there so much evil in the world? Why is there so much hate among nations and individuals? Why is there always the oppressed and the oppressor?

In every generation, in every nation, tribe, and tongue these are commonly asked questions. Sometimes there is an easy explanation, and oftentimes there is not. And sometimes things happen that defy all explanation. This is part of the reality of life on earth.

Why is a child born without arms and legs with no medical explanation to justify this type of birth?

Why would a six-week-old infant contract an infection that would cause permanent blindness?

Why would a young, extremely gifted child be plagued by depression which continues throughout his adult life?

A man in the Bible named Job, perfectly upright in his day, endured the most indescribable suffering known to man, but he remained steadfast and triumphed in the end. He felt alone and forsaken, he felt cheated, he even wished he had never been born. He asked, "Why died I not from the womb? Why did I not give up the ghost when I came out of the belly?" As he sat on the ash heap trying to find relief from itching and painful sores, his frail tiny frame blended in with the ashes. But out of those ashes came beauty because he patiently endured. The Lord gives beauty for ashes, the oil of joy for mourning, the garment of praise for the spirit of heaviness... that *He* might be glorified (Isaiah 61:3).

This book offers a biblical perspective on human suffering and how it is intertwined with us fulfilling our divine purpose, which is to glorify God on the earth.

CHAPTER ONE

Another Day

A bustling day in the city. The familiar sights, the blaring sounds, the nauseating smells. A chorale of camels grunting, oxen bellowing, sheep bleating. The smell of smoke from the bonfire in the distance was nauseating and all too familiar. Merchants, both young and old, displayed their wares with enthusiasm. It was an extremely busy time of the year with commercial activity at its peak. But it was also a time of feasting, and Job's children were all at their brother's house living the good life and drinking wine.

Suddenly Job received horrific news that was unbelievable. Marauding gangs had stolen hundreds of his livestock and killed his servants. Almost simultaneously lightning struck and killed all his sheep and the servants that were with them. Then a hurricane force wind blew in from the wilderness and demolished the house where his children were feasting and, tragically, they were all killed. These events all happened in rapid succession.

CHAPTER TWO

Who is Job?

Job was a billionaire in his day who owned a plethora of livestock and had numerous servants. God characterized Job as a "perfect and upright man," because he was a man of impeccable character and integrity who walked uprightly; shunning all forms of evil. As a highly respected member of the community, he helped the helpless, strengthened the weak, gave hope to the hopeless, and even became a mentor to many. But he lived in fear that one day his children, while drinking, would curse God in their hearts. He was so troubled by the thought, that he continually offered up sacrifices for them after each drinking binge.

The tragic chain of events began suddenly, and quite unexpectedly. Job was devastated. The shock made him tremble. Life had dealt him a terrible blow. In his unspeakable anguish, grief, and consternation he tore his robe, shaved his head, and fell to the ground, saying, *"Naked came I out of my mother's womb, and naked shall I return there, the Lord gave and the Lord has taken away, blessed be the name of the Lord"* (Job 1:21). Job did not sin by blaming God for his loss, rather, he humbled himself and worshipped—albeit in the depth of despair.

Job did not have the slightest clue what had happened to him. He knew only that he walked in the fear of the Lord and always tried to do right. He was unaware of the evil one—the devil, the thief who had stolen his possessions, killed his children, and destroyed his life. We know this, because it is written.

CHAPTER THREE

What's Going On?

But there was more, life was not finished with him yet. He suddenly contracted painful oozing boils from head to toe. He sat on the ash heap scraping himself with stones to find relief and longed for death, while his wife urged him to curse God and die. His three friends heard of his misfortune and came to mourn with him and to comfort him. When they saw his misery, they wept aloud and sat with him in silence for seven straight days. Then Job began to pour out his unrelenting grief in lengthy discourses with his friends, himself, and with God.

Job's apparent fall from grace was sudden and perplexing. His whole life was shattered, and it happened all in one day. In one day, this great man of substance was reduced to a pitiful frame on the ash heap. He tried to find relief for his sores while writhing in pain and discomfort. He was grief-stricken—how could he not be? His mind, no doubt, was bombarded with thoughts. Hadn't he done everything right? Did he not walk in the fear of God, shunning evil? Didn't he continually offer up sacrifices for his children to save them from the wrath of God? He helped and comforted others. Now he needed comfort, but none came, only agonizing physical, mental, and emotional pain and anguish.

CHAPTER FOUR

Questions Without Answers

Why the sudden misfortune? Is this judgment from the Almighty? If so, what had he done to provoke it? Shouldn't God tell him his sin? He desperately wanted answers, but none came.

Yet, here he was, afflicted in body, soul, and spirit, facing the greatest challenge of his life. And he had no answers. No answers. His breath was nauseating to his wife; he became a stranger in his own house. His friends ridiculed him, and he was alienated from his acquaintances. His loved ones turned against him and the young children scorned him. Job went into "why" mode, and began to ask searching questions of the Almighty:

Why died I not from the womb? Why did I not give up the ghost when I came out of the belly? (Job 3:11 NLT).

Why then did you deliver me from my mother's womb? Why didn't you let me die at birth? (Job 10:18 NLT).

He continued to make his case before God in an attempt to justify himself:

Are not my days few, cease then and let me alone that I may take comfort a little before I go whence I shall not return....to the land of darkness and the shadow of death.
(Job 20:21 NLT).

CHAPTER FIVE

Can You Hear Me?

He continued to pour out his complaint unto God, but the heavens seemed like brass:

My soul loathes my life, I will give free course to my complaint, I will speak in the bitterness of my soul. I will say to God, 'do not condemn me, show me why you contend with me'
(Job 10:1,2 NKJV).

My flesh is clothed with worms and clods of dust; my skin is broken, and become loathsome (Job 7:5).

......therefore I will not refrain my mouth, I will speak in the anguish of my spirit, I will complain in the bitterness of my soul (Job 7:11).

Oh that I might have my request, and that God would grant me the thing that I long for? Even that it would please God to destroy me... (Job 6:8).

Oh that I knew where I might find him, that I might come even to his seat, I would order my cause before him and fill my mouth with arguments (Job 23:4).

CHAPTER SIX

Friends

His three friends patiently listened to his rambling and then spoke. Their brand of comfort was brutal. They judged him, rebuked him, ridiculed him, and told him he was reaping what he had sown. They told him that if he was indeed pure and upright, as he portrayed himself to be, he would not have suffered these misfortunes. They even accused him of not taking his own advice as when he counseled others in distress. These know-it-all friends were convinced that they knew why he was aggrieved, stricken, and tormented. Job listened intently and then angrily rebuked them one by one.

> *...I have understanding as well as you; I am not inferior to you...(Job 12:3).*

> *What you know, the same do I know also, I am not inferior unto you (Job 13:2).*

> *Ye are forgers of lies, ye are all physicians of no value, O that ye would altogether hold your peace and it should be your wisdom (Job 13:4).*

> *One should be kind to a fainting friend, but you accuse me without any fear of the Almighty (Job 6:14 NLT).*

Kudos to Job for rebuking these miserable comforters disguised as friends. He was bold and courageous in his own defense, even as they ganged up against him as judge and jury to condemn him. He did not cave under the pressure but was firm in his belief that he was innocent. He continued to mount his defense, going back and forth with his 'fake' friends. 'Fake friends' is not a new concept.

CHAPTER SEVEN

What Happened?

Job's family and friends were aware of the terrible misfortunes that he suffered on that ill-fated day. But did they know what precipitated and predetermined these outcomes? We read in Job Chapter 1:

> *There was a man in the land of Uz, whose name was Job: and that man was perfect and upright and one that feared God and eschewed evil... Now there was a day when the sons of God came to present themselves before the Lord, and Satan came also among them. And the Lord said to Satan, Whence comest thou? Then Satan answered the Lord and said, From going to and fro in the earth, and from walking up and down in it. And the Lord said to Satan, Hast thou considered my servant Job, that there is none like him in the earth, a perfect and an upright man, one that feareth God, and escheweth evil?*
>
> *Then Satan answered the Lord, and said... Doth Job fear God for naught? Hast thou not made a hedge about him, and about his house, and about all that he hath on every side? Thou hast blessed the work of his hands and his substance is increased in the land. But put forth thine hand now, and touch all that he hath, and he will curse thee to thy face. And the Lord said unto Satan,*

Behold, all that he hath is in thy power, only upon himself put not forth thine hand. So Satan went forth from the presence of the Lord.

Again there was a day when the sons of God came to present themselves before the Lord, and Satan came also among them to present himself before the Lord. And the Lord said unto Satan, From whence comest thou? And Satan answered the Lord and said, From going to and fro in the earth and from walking up and down in it. And the Lord said unto Satan, Hast thou considered my servant Job, that there is none like him in the earth, a perfect and an upright man, one that feareth God and escheweth evil? And still he holdeth fast his integrity, although thou movedst me against him, to destroy him without cause. And Satan answered the Lord and said, skin for skin, all that a man hath will he give for his life. But put forth thine hand now and touch his bone and his flesh, and he will curse thee to thy face. So Satan went forth from the presence of the Lord and smote Job with sore boils from the sole of his foot unto his crown" (Job 2:1-7).

CHAPTER EIGHT

What Actually Happened

These events were all precipitated and predetermined by a heavenly discourse to which Job was not privy. He was the sole focus of it, yet he was quite oblivious of it. So were his family and friends. The predetermined outcome of this heavenly discourse was destined to change his life and make it a memorial to God's faithfulness. The obvious here is that things are not always what they appear to be.

How long was Job's affliction? The scriptures are not clear on this, but Bible scholars say it was for a "prolonged period of time." All throughout his ordeal, he constantly lamented his condition and vigorously questioned the justice of the Almighty, but he maintained his integrity and did not sin against God. Was this strength of character, or was it God's amazing grace? Some may think it sinful or inappropriate to question God as Job did. But God was not unhinged by Job's questioning. He never is. He patiently listened to Job's ranting and then gave him a reality check. Did someone say God does not speak?

Then the Lord answered Job from the whirlwind:

Who is this that questions my wisdom with such ignorant words? Brace yourself like a man, because I have some questions for you, and you must answer them. Where were you when I laid the foundations of the earth? Tell me, if you know so much.

Who determined its dimensions and stretched out the surveying line? What supports its foundations, and who laid its cornerstone as the morning stars sang together and all the angels shouted for joy?

Who kept the sea inside its boundaries as it burst from the womb, and as I clothed it with clouds, and wrapped it in thick darkness? For I locked it behind barred gates, limiting its shores. I said, 'This far and no farther will you come. Here your proud waves must stop!'

Have you ever commanded the morning to appear and caused the dawn to rise in the east? Have you made daylight spread to the ends of the earth, to bring an end to the night's wickedness? As the light approaches, the earth takes shape like clay pressed beneath a seal; it is robed in brilliant colors. The light disturbs the wicked and stops the arm that is raised in violence.

Have you explored the springs from which the seas come? Have you explored their depths? Do you know where the gates of death are located? Have you seen the gates of utter gloom? Do you realize the extent of the earth? Tell me about it if you know!

Where does light come from, and where does darkness go? Can you take each to its home? Do you know how to get there? But of course, you know all this! For you were born before it was all created, and you are so very experienced! (God's sense of humor).

Have you visited the storehouses of the snow or seen the storehouses of hail? (I have reserved them as weapons for the time of trouble, for the day of battle and war). Where is the path to the source of light? Where is the home of the east wind?

Who created a channel for the torrents of rain? Who laid out the path for the lightening? Who makes the rain fall on barren land, in a desert where no one lives? Who sends rain to satisfy the parched ground and make the tender grass spring up?

Does the rain have a father? Who gives birth to the dew? Who is the mother of the ice? Who gives birth to the frost from the heavens? For the water turns to ice as hard as rock, and the surface of the water freezes.

Can you direct the movement of the stars—binding the cluster of Pleiades or loosening the cords of Orion? Can you direct the constellations through the seasons or guide the Bear with her cubs across the heavens? Do you know the laws of the universe? Can you use them to regulate the earth?

Can you shout to the clouds and make it rain? Can you make lightning appear and cause it to strike as you direct? Who gives intuition to the heart and instinct to the mind? Who is wise enough to count all the clouds? Who can tilt the water jars of heaven when the parched ground is dry and the soil has hardened into clods?

Can you stalk a prey for a lioness and satisfy the young lions' appetites as they lie in their dens or crouch in the thicket? Who provides food for the ravens when their young cry out to God and wander about in hunger? (Job Chapter 38).

CHAPTER NINE

The Process

The obvious is that the heavenly realm is very much involved in earthly happenings. One demonstration of this is when Jesus told Peter in Luke 22:32 that, "Satan has desired to sift you as wheat." Jesus did not tell Peter that Satan's desire was not granted, because it was. He told him that He had already prayed for him that his faith would not fail. In effect, He made provision for his victory and restoration even before Peter would go through the process.

As witnesses to Jesus' resurrection, Peter and his brethren were going to establish the church, a new phenomenon in that day. God's greater purpose in allowing Satan to afflict Peter was to prepare him for that groundbreaking work. His faith was strengthened, and he was then able to strengthen his brethren. This suggests that, according to the will and purposes of God, Peter had to go through the process. The greatest challenge in our Christian walk is keeping the faith, from start to finish and all in between, because our faith is the enemy's prime target.

CHAPTER TEN

The Process Continued

Another example of heavenly orchestration is Paul in the following:

And lest I should be exalted above measure, through the abundance of the revelations, there was given to me a thorn in the flesh, the messenger of Satan to buffet me, lest I should be exalted above measure (2 Corinthians 12:7).

Paul asked the Lord three times to relieve him of this affliction but God's answer to him was, *"My grace is sufficient for thee."* This was to protect Paul from the spirit of pride and a subsequent fall so that the scriptures would be fulfilled concerning him and all that he had to accomplish for the kingdom of God. In similar circumstances, one might question why God would allow the affliction to continue. It is because the fulfillment of His eternal purposes always takes precedence, and in this case, it was over the inconvenience and discomfort of Paul's 'light' affliction. Meanwhile, however, He provides all the grace that is necessary to not only deal with, but to overcome the challenge. Jesus Christ is the same yesterday, today, and forever.

CHAPTER ELEVEN

You Have No Power Over Me

Then Pilate said to him, *"Are you not speaking to me? Do you not know that I have power to crucify you, and power to release you? Jesus answered: You102*

could have no power at all against me unless it had been given you from above" (John 19:10,11 NKJV).

Jesus' response to Pilate was the fulfillment of Isaiah's prophecy in Chapter 53:7. *"He was oppressed and He was afflicted, yet he opened not his mouth, He was led as a lamb to the slaughter...so He opened not His mouth."* Moreover, it was the fulfillment of God's eternal purposes in his role as the Lamb of God. As powerful as Pilate was, he could do nothing to Jesus except what God's counsel had already predetermined. Satan has no power over the believer except what the believer sanctions by the words of his mouth ("death and life are in the power of the tongue and they that love it shall eat the fruit thereof." Proverbs 8:12), and what God allows for the fulfillment of His eternal purposes.

God's challenge to Satan concerning Job indicates that he was highly favored by God, as a trophy He was proud to display. Satan responded with his own challenge and received a limited license to afflict Job. He was convinced that Job's sudden misfortune would cause him to lose faith and confidence in God. However, Job proved him wrong. He kept his integrity. He did not sin against God.

CHAPTER TWELVE

Faith is the Victory

As Satan was relentless in his pursuit of Job, so Job was relentless in his commitment to God. He never lost faith in who and whose he was. He never lost faith in God. *"....and this is the victory that overcometh the world, even our faith"* (1 John 5:4). We must never lose faith in who and whose we are as sons of God, clothed in the righteousness of Jesus Christ.

Though Job was highly favored by God, this favor did not exclude him from suffering affliction. It did not preempt him from a fiery trial. It did not exempt him from despondency. As with Job, so it is with every born-again Christian because we belong to God. Does God give permission to afflict His own? He does, but it is always with His eternal purposes in mind. It is always for the accomplishment and advancement of His eternal purposes of which we are a part. These purposes involve us becoming mature in Christ because we are destined to reign with Him according to 2 Timothy 2:12 and Revelation 20:6.

If we suffer, we shall also reign with him; if we deny him, he also will deny us. Blessed and holy are those who share in the first resurrection. For them the second death holds no power, but they will be priests of God and of Christ and will reign with him a thousand years (Rev. 20:6 NLT).

CHAPTER THIRTEEN

The Battle Rages

Furthermore, as earthen vessels, we carry this treasure within, the glory of God which is revealed in and through us. The glory of God cannot be seen in the earth except that it is first revealed in and through his earthen vessels. Isaiah prophesied, *"For the earth shall be filled with the glory of the Lord as the waters cover the sea"* (Isaiah 11:9).

Seemingly what happened to Job did not have much to do with Job. He was a pawn, as we all are, in the age-old battle between good and evil, light and darkness. This battle began long before man entered the earthly realm and will continue to rage until Satan is ultimately destroyed by God in the lake of fire. This battle is a fact of life in the earthly realm. God created us as spirit beings housed in a dirt body and then breathed into us the breath of life, making us living entities with a directive to replenish the earth and exercise dominion over it.

The Son of God, Jesus Christ, came as the Son of Man, to restore our spiritual dominion in the earth. He did this through his death, resurrection, and ascension. He is now seated at the right hand of God advocating and making intercession for all who call upon him 24/7. The Man, Christ Jesus, seated at the right hand of Majesty on High, is the basis of man's spiritual authority on the earth. He is our Great High Priest, and He ever lives to make intercession for us.

CHAPTER FOURTEEN

The Living Word

It was in God's eternal purposes that His Word that lives and abides forever, relevant in every age, every generation and every circumstance, would be written and preserved down through the ages so that we would know the truth and be made free from the tyranny of Satan, whom Jesus called a liar and the father of lies. He is the master of deception, and his mission is *to steal, kill and destroy* according to John 10:10. He goes about like a roaring lion seeking whom he may devour. He hates God, and he hates man who is made in the image and likeness of God. Make no mistake about it, he hates all that is good and lovely and true.

In the book of Revelation Chapter 22 he is called the "accuser of the brethren." This is because he accuses us to God, day and night. Not only does he accuse us to God, but he also accuses God to us; then he accuses us to each other; and lastly, he accuses us to ourselves. Doubt, fear, guilt, condemnation, pride, deception, unbelief, unforgiveness, self-righteousness, and so forth are some of the weapons of mass destruction that he uses to wreak havoc on humanity. He said to Eve in the Garden of Eden, "Did God say?" to cast doubt. Then he said, "You shall not surely die," to seed unbelief. He still uses those weapons and many others today. His modus operandi has not changed. *"Be sober, be vigilant, because your adversary the devil, as a roaring lion, walketh about seeking whom he may devour"* (1 Peter 5:8).

CHAPTER FIFTEEN

The Devil's Native Language

He is still casting doubt and suggesting unbelief about everything that God says to us in His Word. He speaks to us in the first person and in our own voice, so we are often deceived into thinking that they are our own thoughts. When we entertain these thoughts, he gains an entrance into our soul; once he has gained an entrance, he torments us with those same thoughts to emit a response. Once we act on those thoughts, he seizes that opportunity to torment us with guilt and condemnation.

Thank God, *"There is therefore now no condemnation to them that are in Christ Jesus who walk not after the flesh but after the spirit"* (Romans 8:1). We are not to be conformed to this world but be transformed by the renewing of our mind. We must renew our mind according to the Word of God because the Word of God is the Mind of God. When we truly know the Mind of God we cannot be deceived.

God watches over His Word to preserve it and perform it. He gave us His Word so we would not "perish for a lack of knowledge," according to Hosea 4:6. He pleads with us in the Book of Proverbs: *"Get wisdom, get understanding, forget it not, neither decline from the words of my mouth.*

Forsake her not and she shall preserve thee, love her and she shall keep thee" Proverbs 4:5-6.

God wants us to know the truth regarding who He is and who we are in Him so we will not be deceived and kept in bondage by the enemy. He wants us to know the truth regarding His will and purposes for our lives.

"Wisdom is the principal thing, therefore get wisdom, and with all thy getting, get understanding" (Prov 4:7).

CHAPTER SIXTEEN

Freedom

Jesus said that if we continue in His Word, then are we His disciples indeed, and we shall know the truth and the truth shall make us free. Free to what? Free to give and receive love, free to forgive and receive forgiveness. Free to believe all that the Word of God says and apply it to our lives so that we can effect change in the earth, thus being the salt and light that the earth needs. Multitudes walk around with their minds blinded by Satan because they do not believe the gospel of the Kingdom. Multitudes of the walking dead are still in the valley of decision; walking but dead because, *"He that hath the Son hath life, but he that hath not the Son of God hath not life"* (1 John 5:12).

God is Jehovah-Jireh—The Lord who provides. God made provision for our healing, deliverance, and restoration while we were still in the loins of Adam (Genesis 3:15). He sent His word to heal us and deliver us from our distresses according to Psalm 107:11. This healing, deliverance and restoration is relevant and active in every generation because the Word of God is relevant and active in every generation. God is a God of purpose and destiny. He wanted the words of Job to be written for a memorial to His faithfulness for the benefit of every generation. He wants us to know of this ancient battle and how to be on the winning side. He also wants us to know of many spiritual truths found in the Book of Job.

CHAPTER SEVENTEEN

Wisdom

Job's lengthy discourses are filled with knowledge, wisdom, and understanding. We catch a glimpse of God's magnificent power as Creator of the universe and many facts of creation. The Book of Job is believed to be the oldest book in the Bible. Centuries before space travel and the National Aeronautics and Space Administration (NASA), Job wrote about the planets Pleaides, Orion, and Arcturus. Long before NASA and astronomy, Job mused about the earth being hung in space, on nothing, and penned these words, *"God stretches the northern sky over empty space and hangs the earth on nothing!"* (Job 26:7 NLT).

Our planet earth is literally suspended in space! It hangs on nothing and rests on nothing. How can that be? According to Hebrews 1:3, *God upholds all things by the word of His power*! Job was made privy to this because God revealed it to him. Daniel 2:28 tells us, *"there is a God that revealeth secrets."*

The truths revealed in the Book of Job are there for our learning. Again, we learn that our struggle is not between us and our neighbor, husband, wife, friend, or boss; but between light and darkness, good and evil. We learn of God's faithfulness, and that our status in life does not exempt us from spiritual realities. We learn that the enemy of God is also the enemy of man, and in this ancient battle the bounty is the souls of men.

CHAPTER EIGHTEEN

Increased Knowledge

During his indescribably painful experience Job wished that his words would be written in stone and preserved forever. He wanted a monument built to his life experiences and carved in a rock forever. He said, *"Oh that my words could be recorded, oh that they could be inscribed on a monument, carved with an iron chisel and filled with lead, engraved forever in the rock"* (Job 19:23 NLT). It sounds like a 'far out' request, but it was not too much for God to grant to His servant Job.

Job got his desire! His words were written in the Rock of Ages! They are inscribed on a monument and that monument is the Word of God which lives and abides forever, and is relevant in every age, generation, and circumstance. The eternal counsel of God predetermined that Job's words would be written in the holy scriptures, and that his life would be a memorial to God's faithfulness.

Indeed, Job was highly favored by God, but it did not exempt him from going through a fiery trial—at the end of which his life was radically transformed, and he declared, *"I have heard of thee by the hearing of the ear but now mine eye seeth thee" (Job 42:5)*. This experience brought Job to a new level of strength, a new level of glory, and a new level of maturity.

After he patiently endured God restored Job and honored him in the eyes of his "fake" friends. Job prayed for them, as God commanded, and he was healed and restored twice as much as he had before. Twice he is mentioned in the book of the Prophet Ezekiel along with Daniel who was "greatly beloved" of God, and Noah, God's friend. But his elevation did not come without refinement. Refinement in the furnace of affliction. If Job had had a preview of what his refining process would look like he probably would have asked for a pass on that. Job's "processing" was for the glory of God and the good of all God's people, it had nothing to do with Job himself. The most challenging problems we face really have nothing to do with us personally but are part of the eternal purposes of God concerning us and the lives of those whom we touch throughout our journey.

In this fiery trial Job received a deeper revelation of the God he thought he knew but really didn't know as he thought. Many times we come through a challenge stronger than before and think that we really know God. Before long a greater challenge comes along and we are stretched to the limit, only to find out that we didn't know Him as we thought, but that He is much greater than our perception of Him. This process repeats itself over and over because it is how we go from strength to strength and glory to glory. Stretching produces growth and growth builds strength and endurance, both of which are essentials on the journey of life.

CHAPTER NINETEEN

Renewal

The Bible says that God chose us in Christ before the foundation of the world, that we should be *"holy and without blame before him in love"* (Ephesians 1:4). In other words, He chose us to become exactly like His Son Jesus Christ, to attain to His spiritual maturity. This "becoming" is the process by which the newborn spirit of Christ in us, which we receive when we become born again, is nurtured into spiritual maturity. This process occurs when we become transformed by the renewing of our minds. We renew our minds by becoming doers of the Word and not hearers only. Only with our lives transformed can we prove that good and acceptable and perfect will of God. This requires a constant yielding to the Holy Spirit who teaches us all things that Jesus taught and guides us into ALL truth.

As earthen vessels in the hands of the potter consistently yielding to the Holy Spirit is vital for the forming and fashioning work with jars of clay. He is the One that molds us into the image of Christ. Paul tells us, *"It is God who works in you both to will and to do of his good pleasure"* (Philippians 2:13*).* Jesus who lives in us wants to reveal Himself in and through us through the work of the indwelling Holy Spirit so that God can be glorified and His purposes in the earth fulfilled through his Body, which we are.

How is this accomplished? It is accomplished by abiding in the vine. Jesus said, *"I am the vine, ye are the branches, abide in me, and I in you. As the branch cannot bear fruit of itself, except it abides in the vine, no more can ye except ye abide in me......for without me ye can do nothing."* (John 15:4,5). This is very clear. How do we abide in the vine? Again, Jesus gives us the answer. *"If ye keep my commandments ye shall abide in my love, even as I have kept my Father's commandments and abide in his love"* (John 15:10). It is by keeping His commandments, and according to 1 John 5:3, "his commandments are not grievous."

Also, we must decrease so that Jesus Christ in us can increase. As He is lifted up in our lives, He draws others to Himself. The world cannot see the risen Christ unless they see Him through His Body here on earth—which we are. But we must indeed be dead to ourselves so that this new life can be manifested in and through us. If there is no dying to self, no decreasing of self, there is no increase or growth of the life of Christ in us.

When we become born again, we receive a new nature, the very nature of God, we are a new creation, and we take on Christ's identity. We must therefore live in and walk out our new identity so that Jesus Christ can be magnified and glorified in our lives. And to the degree that we live in and walk out our new identity, we experience the more than abundant life, the supernatural life that Jesus came to give to us.

This truth cannot be overstated. To abide in the vine, we must die daily, die to self and all that self represents; this 'self' being a god unto itself. Paul put it this way:

> *Likewise reckon ye also yourselves to be dead indeed unto sin but alive unto God through Jesus Christ* (Romans 6:11).

He also said, "*Ye are dead and your life is hid with Christ in God*" (Colossians 3:3).

> *I am crucified with Christ, nevertheless I live, yet not I but Christ liveth in me.* (Galatians 2:20).

Then he said, "*Know ye not that your body is the temple of the Holy Ghost which is in you, which ye have of God, and ye are not your own? For ye are bought with a price...*(1 Corinthians 6:19,20).

CHAPTER TWENTY

Divine Set-Up

Again, as previously stated, it is God who first **wills** and then **performs** His good pleasure in us as we yield to the promptings of the Holy Spirit. It is not by our might, not by our power, nor by our intelligence or innate abilities, but by the Spirit of the Living God. It is in Him that we live, and move, and have our being. We may recall incidents that occurred in our lives which, in hindsight, seemed to be part of a larger tapestry. And throughout the Word of God, we see that oftentimes adverse circumstances endured by individuals were all part of God's divine plan in bringing them to Himself for the fulfillment of His divine purposes. Let's explore a few.

Saul went looking for his father's lost donkeys when he met the Prophet Samuel to whom God had already given instructions concerning him. Samuel anointed him as king of Israel and his life was radically changed that day. David was foreordained by God to be the king of Israel and Saul filled the gap until the fullness of time came for David to ascend the throne. This scenario of the lost donkeys was a set up by God for Saul's date with destiny.

Joseph's dream incited his hateful brothers to throw him in a pit to die. They later changed their minds and sold him into slavery. As a slave he was wrongly accused of sexual assault by his master's wife and ended up in prison. While in the prison the king had a terrifying dream and summoned Joseph to interpret the dream. The king was so pleased with his interpretation that he immediately elevated him to second place in the kingdom. When a severe famine came upon the land Joseph was in the right place at the right time in the right position to save his entire family from death by starvation. Joseph's response to his fearful and guilt-ridden brothers was, *"As for you, ye thought evil against me, but God meant it unto good, to bring to pass, as it is this day, to save much people alive"* (Genesis 50:20). Here again, Joseph's misfortune at the hand of his evil brothers was another scenario set up by divine providence for the fulfillment of God's eternal purposes. This was the family through which the promised Redeemer would come.

Daniel's jealous subordinates conspired against him, petitioning the king to make a decree that was unfavorable to Daniel's religion, namely, for the next thirty days no prayer was to be made to any god or man but the king. Daniel continued his daily prayer routine in defiance of the king's command and was thrown into the lions' den. God miraculously protected him from the ferocious lions and those who plotted against him were thrown in themselves and mangled by the hungry lions. The king then made a decree:

I make a decree, that in every dominion of my kingdom men tremble and fear before the God of Daniel; for he is the living God, and steadfast forever, and his kingdom that which shall not be destroyed, and his dominion shall be even unto the end. He delivered and rescueth, and he worketh signs and wonders in heaven and in earth, who hath delivered Daniel from the power of the lions (Daniel 6:26,27).

Daniel's ordeal was a divine set up to glorify the God of heaven among all people so that they would know that He is the only true and living God, able to deliver like no other. Through Daniel's miraculous triumph over the ferocious lions, the king and all citizens of the kingdom feared the God of Daniel who showed Himself stronger than any other god, glorifying Himself among the heathen. Also, the king, who himself was a god to the people, and a god unto himself, found out that there is One greater that is not merely called god but is indeed the true and living God, before whom he was forced to humble himself.

Shadrach, Meshach, and Abednego defied the king's command by refusing to worship the golden image. It so enraged the king that they were thrown, fully clothe, into a blazing fiery furnace heated seven times above the normal temperature; even the soldiers who threw them into the furnace were killed by the scorching heat. *"Did not we cast three men bound into the midst of the fire?"* The king asked his counsellors in utter dismay, *"Look, I see four men loose walking in the midst of the fire!"* (Daniel 3:24,25).

They walked out of the fiery furnace unharmed with clothes and hair intact without even the smell of smoke. This miraculous deliverance prompted the heathen king to first bless the God of Shadrach, Meshach and Abednego saying, *"Blessed be the God of Shadrach, Meshach, and Abednego, who hath sent his angel, and delivered his servants that trusted in him, and have changed the king's word, and yielded their bodies, that they might not serve nor worship any god, except their own God. Therefore, I make a decree, that every people, nation, and language which speak anything amiss against the God of Shadrach, Meshach, and Abednego, shall be cut in pieces and their houses shall be made a dunghill; because there is no other God that can deliver after this sort"* (Daniel 3:28 and 29).

Because these men defied the king's order, the king who was a god unto himself, found out that the God of Shadrach, Meshach and Abednego was a God like no other who could deliver like no other. He was forced to humble himself under the mighty hand of God. God used this incident to make His name and mighty power known to all. His glory was revealed among the heathen according to His eternal purposes. This also was a divine set up so that His name could be glorified among the heathen, it was the greater purpose for Shadrach, Meshach and Abednego's ordeal.

Baby Moses was rescued from the water and grew up in Pharaoh's court where he learned the culture of the Egyptians. After killing an Egyptian, he feared for his life and quickly escaped to the land of Midian. While shepherding in the desert God commanded him to go before Pharaoh and tell him to let his people go. There is no doubt that the "seeming" misfortunes of Moses' life all prepared him for his divine assignment to bring the children of Israel out of Egypt. It was not by chance that he was rescued from the water and brought up in Pharaoh's court.

It was not by chance that he killed the Egyptian and ended up in the desert where he had a divine encounter with the God of his fathers. When he brought the children of Israel out of Egypt the Name of God was glorified far and wide, among the heathen nations. All the pain that he encountered was for the greater good, the fulfillment of God's eternal purposes.

Reading of these events in hindsight we see the big picture. In every instance God had already pre-arranged the outcome for the fulfillment of His eternal purposes. He made provision for what was ahead long before Moses, Saul, Joseph, and Daniel were put on assignment, the same happened with Job. I believe it works the same for us.

Since God knows the end from the beginning, He already knows what's going to happen, in every situation, so like a loving father, He goes before us and makes provision for our victory over circumstances and our restoration; and He determines the means by which we would be restored. The means can be perplexing to our finite minds, but He tells us in Isaiah 55:9 *"My thoughts are not your thoughts, neither are your ways my ways."*

When God removed His hedge of protection from Job, He knew that he would be faithful to the end while maintaining his integrity; and He also knew that His grace would be sufficient to see him through the challenge. Most importantly, He knew that Job's words were going to be written in "The Rock" so that His people down through the ages could learn of His faithfulness, and through the scriptures find comfort and hope. This was the greater good, the fulfillment of His eternal purposes.

CHAPTER TWENTY-ONE

Another Plan

Because we serve an unchanging God, we can be assured that even before we find ourselves in the fire, His plan of restoration is already at work. This was evident in the Garden of Eden when Adam and Eve sinned. God told Satan that the seed of the woman would bruise his head; that seed was Jesus Christ who was to come, born of a woman. We can also be assured that He has already provided the grace sufficient to, not only meet the challenge, but to overcome it.

As Jacob grieved over his son Joseph, whom he thought was dead, God knew that Jacob would see his son again, but Jacob continued to grieve as someone with no hope and 'refused to be comforted'. It pained the Father's heart to see Jacob aggrieved for his son, even knowing that he would see him again, but His divine purposes overrule in every situation; His Word is forever settled in heaven. We know that it pained the Father's heart because Isaiah tells us, *"In all their affliction he was afflicted, and the angel of his presence saved them: in his love and in his pity he redeemed them, and he bare them, and carried them all the days of old"* (Isaiah 63:9).

Though He felt compassion for Jacob in his grief, and for Joseph in his troubles, His eternal purposes concerning them prevailed. God sustained them until the time their deliverance came. David said, *"Weeping may endure for a night, but joy comes in the morning"* (Psalm 30:5). Joy did come in the morning for Jacob and Joseph, but only after they had gone through the process, as grievous as it was, for the advancement of God's eternal purposes. In this case, to preserve life and the line through which the promised Messiah would come. Joseph and Jacob's suffering was for the greater good.

With Saul, the children of Israel had rejected God as their king and insisted they wanted a king like the nations around them. God forewarned them through the Prophet Samuel that the king would severely oppress them, but they insisted. God gave them their desire and they learned the hard way. If we insist on having something badly enough, God will sometimes give it to us. Lessons learned the hard way are the ones that are most impactful. King Saul oppressed the people until he was killed in battle through his own disobedience. The Word of God was fulfilled according to Samuel and opened the way for David, the chosen one, to sit on the throne.

As none of these events had anything to do with the main characters but was part of God's eternal purposes, so with Job, so with us. It is God's will that our faith be tried with fire. It is God's will that the trial of our faith may be found to result in praise and glory and honor at the revelation of Jesus Christ. But God is the one who sovereignly determines the duration and intensity of the fire. Because it is in His eternal purposes that we rule and reign with Christ and every day of our lives He is preparing us for just that. *"Behold, I have refined thee, but not with silver, I have chosen thee in the furnace of affliction"* (Isaiah 48:10).

CHAPTER TWENTY-TWO

The Same Strategy

We are partakers of Christ's suffering according to 1 Peter 4:13, *"Beloved, think it not strange concerning the fiery trial which is to try you, as though some strange thing happened unto you but rejoice, inasmuch as ye are partakers of Christ's sufferings."* After Paul was stoned and left for dead he returned with Barnabas to the cities where they were persecuted *"confirming the souls of the disciples and exhorting them to continue in the faith, and that we must through much tribulation enter into the kingdom of God"* (Acts 14:22). Maybe Paul was reminding the disciples of what Jesus had said to them, *"In the world you shall have tribulation but be of good cheer, I have overcome the world"* (John 16:33).

I believe that our fiery trials are all part of God's divine plan in bringing us to Himself so that we might know Him whom to know is life eternal. What is life eternal? It is the God life, the Jesus life, the Zoe life; it is the life and life more abundant that Jesus came to give us, it is supernatural life. The challenges we face, whether in the form of persecution, tribulation, trials, or disappointments are part of living in a fallen world. In addition, we have a free will to choose good or evil, and God never violates this will. We are then forced to live with our wrong choices because of the natural law of sowing and reaping.

Another factor is our thought life. "For as a man thinks in his heart so is he." Moreover, the words that we speak either bring death or life. *"Death and life are in the power of the tongue and they that love it shall eat the fruit thereof"* (Proverbs 18:21). Disobedience to spiritual laws also brings challenges, and then of course we have an adversary, the devil, who stands near to resist us at every turn.

God does not create these challenges, but He uses them for His divine purposes. He makes them work together for our good so that His name would be glorified in our lives according to the fulfillment of His eternal purposes as in the case of Daniel, Joseph, Moses, and countless others.

CHAPTER TWENTY-THREE

Guaranteed Victory

God promised the children of Israel that He would bring them out of Egypt into a good land flowing with milk and honey. But this was the same land inhabited by the Amorites, the Hittites, the Perizzites, and the Canaanites, whom He promised to drive out from before them. He also commissioned Joshua to go and "possess" the land because He had already given it to them. He brought them into enemy territory.

Similarly, when we come out of the bondage of the world (Egypt) and receive Christ we also come into a good land, but it is also a land inhabited by the enemies of our souls, which God Himself will drive out from us as we yield to Him. These enemies are both internal and external. The land flowing with milk and honey is the indwelling presence of God, He is in us and thus always with us. His sweet presence is ever with us flowing into, through and out of us. It is flowing because it is a river of life, eternal life, God life, Jesus life, Zoe life, supernatural life, overcoming life. It is life in the overflow of God's goodness and love, mercy, grace, and abundance. It is a good land.

In this land, He has given us the authority to *"tread upon serpents and scorpions and over all the power of the enemy"* (Luke 10:19). In this land

He said we shall have tribulation but be of good cheer because He has overcome the world, thus we overcome in Him. In this land we have the Name of Jesus and the power of the Holy Spirit, we have God in us, with us, and for us, thus we have everything that we need to be victorious over our circumstances. *"Nay in all these things we are more than conquerors through him that loved us"* (Romans 8:37).

CHAPTER TWENTY-FOUR

The Mystery Revealed

The Lord hath appeared of old unto me, saying, *"Yea, I have loved thee with an everlasting love: therefore with lovingkindness have I drawn thee"* Jeremiah 31:3.

God uses lovingkindness to draw us into relationship with Him to effectuate partnership for the accomplishment and advancement of His purposes on the earth. He sent each of us here with and for a purpose that we can adequately fulfill only if we are in partnership with Him. How does this work? When we go through struggles, He makes Himself real to us in the struggle, walks us through, and brings us out, in *His* time. When we come out of that struggle, we have a deeper revelation of the God we are serving. *"For thus saith the high and lofty one that inhabiteth eternity, whose name is Holy; I dwell in the high and holy place with him also that is of a contrite and humble spirit, to revive the spirit of the humble, and to revive the heart of the contrite ones"* (Isaiah 57:15).

The mystery yet remains for some—why did God allow Job, a perfect and upright man, to suffer so terribly? Some have said Job brought the suffering upon himself because of harboring fear which gave Satan an open door to afflict him.

Others have said this was for Job to learn humility. Still, others have said, it is a mystery, we don't know why the righteous suffer. Down through the ages many have had the same query and settled it in their hearts that it is a mystery, thus we will never have the answer until we get to heaven. I suggest that when looked at it from God's perspective and the fulfillment of His eternal purposes, it is not so mysterious.

It is not a mystery when we consider the fact that God created us for **His** glory. We are here first and foremost for the glory of God. All things were created by Jesus and for Jesus and that includes us human beings. God created us for fellowship with Him and to be in partnership with Him. In this partnership God's glory is revealed through us earthen vessels. This is God's original plan according to Isaiah 43:7 which says, *"Even everyone that is called by my name for I have created him for my glory, I have formed him, yea I have made him."*

I would deem Job's experience a "Knowledge of the Highest" course. From this experience he gained a new perspective on God. The same God he had worshipped for so long but did not truly know. He received glimpses of the utter majesty of God. He experienced the faithfulness of God. He also discovered that God is just. Though he complained and repeatedly bemoaned his birth, he did not curse God as Satan said he would, and as his wife said he should, but maintained his integrity. He was dogged in his faith. Through many doubts, fears, and unanswered questions he maintained his position in God. Many have spoken of the "patience" of Job, but I suggest that the "faith" of Job is more accurate. Showing tremendous endurance, he resolutely affirmed and reaffirmed his intent to remain faithful to God saying:

Though he slay me yet will I trust him... (Job 13:15).

All the while my breath is in me, and the spirit of God is in my nostrils, my lips shall not speak wickedness, nor my tongue utter deceit (Job 27:3,4).

My righteousness I hold fast, and will not let it go, my heart shall not reproach so long as I live (Job 27:6).

Even now my witness is in heaven, my advocate is there on high. My friends scorn me but I pour out my tears to God (Job 16:20).

From Job's experience we learn, among other things, that God is faithful. For some of us we have personally learned of His faithfulness, and we are encouraged by Job's unwavering faith; for others, we are challenged by it. We learn that God is just. He is the Judge of all the earth and His judgment is just and righteous. We learn that God takes pleasure in His people, as He did in Job, and was proud to display him before all of creation. Yet, this type of honor comes with a price. Job's weeping endured for a night, a long one, but joy came in the morning, as promised in the Word of God. *"Weeping may endure for a night but joy comes in the morning"* (Psalm 30:5).

So, when we consider the suffering of Job and his end, we see that God is faithful and just. We also see that the fulfillment of His eternal purposes takes precedence. This is the high calling to which He has called us. Job's life was to be a memorial to the justice and faithfulness of God. He was, is and forever will be glorified in the life of Job, on the earth, and among the heathen. Job's life was etched forever in the Rock of Ages. Multitudes down through the ages have found solace and strength reading the Book of Job. Many were encouraged in their faith to keep trusting in God against all odds. Millions have been encouraged to 'fight the good fight of faith' as Paul admonished. They have seen and experienced the faithfulness of our God, Creator of all the ends of the earth. Then life is never the same.

Things may happen that shake us to the core. So much is beyond our finite knowledge; mainly because we only know what we know, and we don't know what we don't know. Thankfully, we serve a God that knows all, sees all, and is all powerful. Therefore, with confidence we can cast our burdens and concerns upon Him knowing that He cares for us.

Truthfully, we are born spiritually dead, dead unto God and dead unto righteousness. Hence the reason Jesus said, *"Ye must be born again"* (John 3:3). As we were born physically to enter the natural world, so we must be born again spiritually to enter the kingdom of God, to be alive unto God and righteousness once again. Because in our natural birth we're born spiritually dead we must have a spiritual rebirth to be alive unto God and righteousness once again. We were spiritually alive (alive unto God) in the Garden before Adam sinned. It is when we are spiritually reborn that our spiritual eyes and ears are opened, our tongues are loosed, our feet and ankle bones receive strength, and our withered hands are once again stretched out unto God.

With eyes opened we "see" Jesus high and lifted up and our need of a Savior; with ears opened we "hear" the joyful sound of His calling. With our tongues loosed we sing and praise the Lord Most High. With our lame feet strengthened we dance unto the Lord, and with our withered hands stretched out we lift them up in praise and adoration unto the great God, the only true and living God. Only when we are spiritually reborn and alive unto God and unto righteousness can we experience the righteousness, peace, and joy of the kingdom of God.

I believe, just as Job's life was written, so our lives are also being written. Paul spoke of us as "living epistles—known and read of all men." Many may never read a Bible, but they will read the Christian. This is why Jesus said, *"Let your light so shine before men that they may see your good works and glorify your Father which is in heaven"* (Matthew 5:16). So, when we experience situations that are perplexing to us and cannot be explained away, let us remember that the Most High God has a higher purpose for everything He allows, and everything He does. He is a God of purpose and destiny. Everything He does or allows is with His eternal purposes in mind which takes precedence over everything else.

Even when He corrects His children, it is redemptive because of the great love that He has for us. A loving parent would not allow his child to continue down a path of destruction but would lovingly restrain him, even if it meant applying strong and painful discipline. We are God's dear children, and He loves and cares for us all. Paul says about Jesus that, as our great high priest, He is touched with the feeling of our infirmities.

When we don't understand, when it doesn't make sense, when it is more than we can fathom, let us remember that our purpose on the earth is to glorify the God who created us for ***His*** glory, who formed us and breathe into us the breath of life. Let us remember that as we are partakers of Christ sufferings we shall also share in His glory. It should also encourage us to know that God is closest to us in our broken places. *"The Lord is nigh unto them that are of a broken heart and saves such as be of a contrite spirit"* (Psalm 34:18).

CHAPTER TWENTY-FIVE

Counted Trustworthy

God is the source of everything. Man in and of himself is unable to do anything because it is in God that we live and move and have our being. All intelligence, all beauty, all wisdom, all knowledge and understanding emanate from the God who created the Universe. Individually and collectively, we are an expression of this Supreme Consciousness whom we call God. God made us in His image and likeness. This likeness was lost when Adam disobeyed. Jesus Christ came to restore us to that likeness; hence we receive a new nature when we are born again, we are a new creature in Christ Jesus. As a new creature we are joined to the Lord and one spirit with Him, once again we have His nature and likeness, once again we have the power of choice.

We have control through our thought life and the choices we make every day. We also have control through our obedience to God, the One who created us and put us on this earth. He lovingly said, *"If ye be willing and obedient ye shall eat the good of the land"* (Isaiah 1:19). So, we choose the 'good of the land' by our loving obedience to the Word of God. God rewards obedience.

Again, back to Job. Why did God subject Job to such terrible suffering even though he was perfect and upright? I have often wondered about that. I agree that Job's fearfulness opened a door for Satan to enter his life, for he himself said, *"For the thing which I greatly feared is come upon me, and that which I was afraid of is come unto me"* (Job 3:25). But that is only one piece of the puzzle. I believe that Isaiah 46:10 is the ultimate answer that answers all the unanswered questions.

Declaring the end from the beginning and from ancient times the things that are not yet done, saying, My counsel shall stand, and I will do all my pleasure.

This is very telling. It shows us that from the very beginning, or even before the beginning, God had the entire plan laid out, from the beginning to the end; everything He would do, and everything He would allow. He would create man with a free will, give Him dominion over the earth, and partner with Him to accomplish His eternal purposes on the earth. In God's fore-knowledge He knew what would happen to Job and He predetermined to use it for His glory and for Job's ultimate good. He is Jehovah Jireh, the Lord who provides, so He goes before us, and makes provision for our restoration. God is a God of purpose, and He created all things with and for purpose. Consequently, the fulfillment of His eternal purposes takes precedence over everything else as stated earlier, including the paths we trod in the journey of life and the fulfillment of our God-given destiny. God created, formed, and made us for His glory.

Even everyone that is called by my name; for I have created him for my glory, I have formed him; yea I have made him" (Isaiah 43:7).

CHAPTER TWENTY-SIX

Modern Jobs

Fanny J Crosby became blind when she was six weeks old, yet grew up to become a missionary, poet, and lyricist, and died at the rich old age of 94. She writes in her autobiography:

When I was six weeks of age a slight cold caused an inflammation of the eyes, which appeared to demand the attention of the family physician; but he not being at home, a stranger was called. He recommended the use of hot poultices, which ultimately destroyed the sense of sight.

I have always believed from my youth to this very moment that the good Lord, in his infinite mercy, by this means consecrated me to the work that I am still permitted to do. When I remember his mercy and lovingkindness, when I have been blessed above the common lot of mortals; and when happiness has touched the deep places of my soul, how can I repine?

Did God make her blind? No, He did not, He didn't have to. He created her and knew what gifts and talents were entrusted to her and how best His kingdom purposes would be accomplished through her, and those whom she would bless throughout her lifetime. "*Known unto God are all His works from the beginning of the world*" (Acts 15:18). So, He allowed it to happen and used it for the advancement of His kingdom purposes. The lesson here is that when a soul is fully committed to God there is no limitation because there are no limitations in God.

Without any medical explanation, Nick Vujicic was born without arms and legs. His parents accepted him and encouraged him. I would imagine, just from the outside looking in, that his life was a challenge. After a suicide attempt at age 10 and overcoming many obstacles, he went on to be a husband and father of three, a world-renowned evangelist, motivational speaker, and international best-selling author.

He writes in his book, *Be the Hands and Feet*, "If God can use a man without arms and legs to be His hands and feet, then He will certainly use any willing heart!"

Why was Nick born without arms and legs? This was already in God's predeterminate counsel, or it would not have happened. Nick is the instrument that God chose to use to provide blessing and restoration for multitudes with his unique God-given gifts and talents. He is also used to encourage others with the same handicap. Who can better encourage someone but someone who is or has been in similar circumstances? Through Nick's amazing life and "seeming" imperfections God is glorified all over the world. Our God is truly amazing! The lesson here again is that in Christ, there are no limitations. Paul said, *"I can do all things through Christ who strengthens me"* Philippians 4:19.

Richard Smallwood, another prolific songwriter, and musician, has blessed millions all over the world with his musical gift. It ministers strength, comfort, joy and peace; the warmth of the Holy Spirit and the love of God comes through his music. He just recently shared in his autobiography, *Total Praise*, that he battled with depression from a very young age, even twice contemplating suicide. While searching out a painless way to do this, he inadvertently called the suicide hotline, and his plan was averted. So, all the while he was producing highly anointed music that was changing hearts and lives everywhere, he was battling fierce demons of depression.

Certainly, God foreknew that his life would be plagued by depression, but as he remained faithful, God shewed His mighty power in him. It reminds us that God's presence is sustaining and will see us through any trial if we do not quit in our minds. Paul tells us that greater is He that is *in* us than he that is in the world. The greater One lives in us. So, at 70+ years old Richard is still giving glory to God as he shares his life experience with others with the same challenges.

These three individuals, despite their handicaps, accomplished a great deal in their lifetimes, despite their limitations. They accomplished much more than many who did not have such limitations. What made the difference?

God inhabits eternity. He sees the past, present and future all at once. He is outside of all three, looking in. Modern thinking points us to our "purpose" as being our career. I strongly disagree with this assessment. I believe there is a higher purpose for our lives which supersedes all others. Paul calls this "the high calling of God in Christ Jesus." Hence when we find our higher purpose in God, all others flow naturally.

Our supreme purpose, as stated in the scriptures, is to know God and Jesus Christ whom He sent for our redemption, and then by spiritual transformation, become His witnesses. Here begins the journey of discovery when we come to a **saving** knowledge of Jesus Christ, the Son of God, the Savior of all mankind. At that point we receive the very nature of God, we become a new creature in Christ Jesus. At that point we are delivered from the power of Satan unto God. We are delivered from the kingdom of darkness and translated into the kingdom of God's dear Son. The journey continues with our being conformed into the image of Christ as that new life is nurtured in us through the knowledge and application of the Word of God.

CHAPTER TWENTY-SEVEN

Getting to Know Him

As we grow in the knowledge of God, grace and peace are multiplied. As grace and peace are multiplied, we go from strength to strength and glory to glory. As we grow in grace and in the knowledge of God becoming doers of the Word, we reflect the glory of the risen Christ and God Himself is glorified. And this is the purpose for which we were created. Repeatedly in the gospels Jesus tells us that we are to lose our lives in this world that we might find it in Him. *"For whosoever will save his life shall lose it, but whosoever shall lose his life for my sake and the gospel's, the same shall save it"* (Mark 8:35).

This is mentioned several times in the gospels: twice in Matthew, twice in Luke, and once in John, for emphasis and to underscore its importance. He wants us to meditate on this and grasp what it means to lose our life in this world and to find it in Him while seeking revelation from the Holy Spirit. Jesus said that we are to be willing to lay down our lives for the brethren, even as He laid down His life for us. This means putting others first if it would bring glory to God, it means esteeming others better than ourselves, making the necessary sacrifices so that the Name of God would be glorified.

It is a deliberate and strong acknowledgement of our new identity in Christ. Now we are no longer our own but we have been bought with a price. It is no longer we who live but Christ who lives in us. It is a decreasing of our former identity (the old man) and an increasing of our new identity in Christ (the new man). It is a deliberate everyday reckoning of the old man dead, and our members as instruments of righteousness unto God.

A byproduct of being tried in the fire, as Job was, is the restoration of the luster which we have from being in union with Christ. Prolonged exposure to life causes us to become tarnished and dull, like precious jewelry would over time. Then the glory of God is obscured as we become lukewarm to the things of God, but the glory of Christ shines brighter when we are restored. Polishing restores the shine because it involves friction; this friction comes in the form of trials, tribulations, persecutions, disappointments, and other problems. Moreover, enduring the fiery trials stretches us, thus increasing our capacity for the things of God. Listen to what our Heavenly Father says concerning His jewels: those who love and fear Him.

Then they that feared the Lord spake often one to another, and the Lord hearkened, and heard it, and a book of remembrance was written before him for them that feared the Lord, and that thought upon his name. And they shall be mine, saith the Lord of hosts, in that day when I make up my jewels" (Malachi 3:16-17).

God created us for His glory and those of us that are His reflect His glory. As the moon has no light of its own but reflects the light of the sun, so we have no light of our own but reflect the light of the SON who is the Light of the world. As our earth needs the sun to sustain life, so the earthen vessels need the Son to sustain life. No physical/natural life on earth without the sun, no spiritual life without the Son.

The account of Job affirms that there is a spiritual component to our lives as children of God. It also affirms that destiny and purpose are tied up in this spiritual component. This spiritual component is the guiding force in our journey of life and cannot be ignored. It dictates outcomes, and it tells us that even though man is a sovereign being, his sovereignty is indeed subject to the sovereignty of God. It also reveals to us that things are not always what they appear to be and may even sometimes explain circumstances that defy explanation.

CHAPTER TWENTY-EIGHT

The Ultimate Revelation

Friends, this is our overarching purpose —overriding all other purposes regardless of how noble—to know the true and living God and the One whom He sent for our redemption, Jesus Christ, and to make Him known. We begin to find our true life in this world when we come into a **saving** (emphasis mine) knowledge of Jesus Christ for *"He who hath the Son hath life but he who hath not the Son of God hath not life"* (1 John 5:12).

This is the whole purpose of man. I believe the paths are laid out for us before we make our entrance into this life. It is true that we enter this life without any personal input or preferences. We had no control over where we were born, our parents, or the circumstances surrounding our birth. If we were given a choice many of us would have chosen differently from the lot we were apportioned. What a thought! Strangely though, as we learn to walk, talk, work, and play we develop the mindset that we are in total control of our destiny and determine *all* the outcomes. Do we really?

This is only partially true. There is One who sometimes overrules our best laid plans for the fulfillment of His eternal purposes of which we are a part. We sometimes find ourselves in circumstances that are totally beyond our control, though the challenge here is how we respond to them. Thankfully, the grace of God operating in our lives empowers us for each challenge. And with each challenge we are stretched to receive a deeper revelation of who He is. Paul said, *"Thanks be unto God which always causeth us to triumph in Christ..."* (2 Corinthians 2:14). God, the Creator, sent us to this earth on a mission.

That mission cannot be successfully completed without following the leading of the One who sent us on the mission. The whole process can be disruptive at times because we generally have our own agendas that top the list of things to do and accomplish. But wholly following after Jesus can sometimes mean delaying or putting aside our own aspirations, and subjugating our will to the sovereign will of God. This is a choice that we make. God created us with the ability to choose, and then gave us choices.

The first choice challenge Adam received was to obey or to disobey God's command. He disobeyed and we were all damned and on our way to hell for eternity. Every day we are faced with the same challenge. Because the Word of God is unchanging and unchangeable, man became separated from God on that fateful day he chose to disobey God's command. He obeyed Satan instead of God and thus took on his nature.

This may seem harsh, but actions do have consequences and God, in His great love, and knowing the end from the beginning, gave man boundaries for his own preservation. This underscores the importance of obedience. In our modern day culture, many think that the grace of God absolves us of the responsibility of loving obedience to God.....heresy! God said through Samuel the prophet, *"to obey is better than sacrifice"* (1 Samuel 15:22). Jesus said to His disciples, *"If you love me keep my commandments"* (John 14:15). Someone once said, "Obedience is heaven's first law." I agree. It was the first explicit commandment given in the Garden of Eden. Because obedience is so important, even Jesus, *"Though he were a Son, yet learned he obedience by the things which he suffered"* (Hebrews 5:8).

Did Jesus need to learn obedience for Himself? I think not. He said, *"The Father hath not left me alone for I do always those things that please him"* (John 8:29). In other words, Jesus was always obedient to the Father. As a man, and the last Adam, Jesus had the nature of God, He was God in the flesh. As babes in Christ, we must learn obedience which does not come naturally to us. So, like Christ, we learn obedience by the things which we suffer, He is our example.

It is a fact that babies do not automatically obey what they are told, they must be taught to obey commands. Did Jesus need to learn it? I think not, but He came to show us the way. Firstly, because He is our example, and secondly, because it is part of the process of our being conformed into the image of Christ. The first test of obedience was given to Adam, the first man, in the Garden of Eden. He failed the test and the penalty for his disobedience came upon the entire human race. Then Jesus, the last Adam who came from heaven, obeyed, and everyone who receives Him receives the reward of His obedience, eternal life, right here and now, not at the time of death.

Simply put, when we choose to obey God, we are choosing life and blessing. When we choose to disobey God as a lifestyle, we choose death and cursing. *"I call heaven and earth to record this day against you, that I have set before you life and death, blessing and cursing: therefore choose life, that both you and your seed may live"* (Deuteronomy 30:19). God wants us to live, and He tells us how.

Making the choice is an act of our sovereign will. We are fully engaged in making choices every day, it is how we are made and how we live. Because Adam chose to disobey God, death and cursing was passed down to all humanity. Jesus Christ, the last Adam, obeyed God and life and blessing was passed down to all who receive Him as Lord and Savior.

When the disciples came to Jesus rejoicing that the devils were subject unto them, He told them, *"Rejoice not that the spirits are subject unto you, but rather rejoice that your names are written in heaven"* (Luke 10:20). Thus showing us that it is far more important to have our names written in heaven than that the devils are subject unto us. Jesus already defeated the devil for us so that we could spend our time and energy on emulating Him. The battle truly is the Lord's.

CHAPTER TWENTY-NINE

Life of Abundance

Becoming like Christ is more than simply living our best life now, or just enjoying everyday life, even though these are quite noble and available for us to do. After all, Jesus came to give us life and life more abundantly; this is life in the overflow of God's love, grace, mercy, peace, goodness, forgiveness, provision, protection, and abundance. It is supernatural life, the life that Adam and Eve enjoyed in the Garden.

But how do we experience this more abundant life? We experience this life by abiding in Christ. A branch has no life apart from the vine; hence Jesus used this illustration to emphasize the importance of abiding in Him.

I am the vine, ye are the branches. As the branch cannot bear fruit of itself, except it abides in the vine, no more can ye, except ye abide in me" (John 15:5,4).

Some expect to experience the more than abundant life that Jesus provides without abiding in Him, but it is impossible to experience the righteousness, peace, and joy of the kingdom without staying connected to the King. Staying connected to the King means being led by the Holy

Spirit as we humble ourselves under the mighty hand of God.

It means being a "doer" of the Word and not a hearer only, it means walking in obedience to the Word of God. When we stay connected to the King we will walk in love as dear children of God, we will walk in the light as He is in the light, we will walk in truth, and we will walk circumspectly toward those that are not in the faith. We will continually reckon ourselves dead unto sin but alive unto righteousness, and alive unto God through Jesus Christ.

It is also acknowledging the sovereignty of God's will over our own will and allowing the Word of God to transform us. The Word of God has the power to transform us because it is a living and powerful entity. This transformation occurs when we renew our minds according to the Word by becoming a doer of the Word. It means being in submission to the good, acceptable, and perfect will of God for our lives every day of our lives. It is redeeming the time because the days are evil, walking in the Spirit so we will not fulfill the lusts of the flesh.

Paul reminds us that, *"All that will live godly in Christ Jesus shall suffer persecution"* (2 Tim 3:12). David says to us in Psalm 34:19, *"Many are the afflictions of the righteous but the Lord delivers him out of them all."* Jesus also admonished His disciples, *"In the world you shall have tribulation but be of good cheer I have overcome the world"* (John 16:33).

Persecution and tribulation can take many forms. Therefore, Jesus Christ came to give us, not only life but life more abundantly; and what is that exactly? It is supernatural life, overcoming life, God life, Jesus life, Zoe life. It is living above all the circumstances of life. More abundant life does not mean a trouble-free life, it means rising above the circumstances and triumphing over them in every way through the power of Christ that is in us. It is life remaining focused on the things of God because therein lies the power to live above the circumstances, and the power to overcome.

Triumph does not necessarily mean winning the race, but it certainly means reaching the finish line. Jesus already won for us and gave us the Holy Spirit so we can endure to the end and reach the finish line. Paul talked about finishing the course and keeping the faith. Jesus Christ has given us the authority to overcome every challenge we face by the power of the Holy Spirit.

Job started off as having a good report. But after his extended trial he was even more highly regarded by God. God rebuked his know-it-all, miserable friends who showed him no mercy, and commanded them to take an offering to Job to offer up for them and pray for them so that they could be healed. God honored Job in the eyes of his friends who condemned him without mercy and judged him unrighteously.

After all that Job experienced, he said to the Almighty, *"I have heard of thee by the hearing of the ear, but now mine eye seeth thee"* (Job 42:5). Job declared during his ordeal, *"But as for me, I know that my Redeemer lives, and he will stand upon the earth at last. And after my body has decayed, yet in my body I will see God. I will see him for myself, I will see him with my own eyes"* (Job 19:25-27). Job had stubborn faith.

When we become spiritually mature, in the midst of our fiery furnace we will say like Job, "Though he slay me yet will I trust him"; or like Paul, "I know whom I have believed and I am persuaded that he is able;" or like Esther, "If I perish I perish;" or like the three Hebrew boys who said, "Be it known unto thee O king, that we will not serve thy gods nor worship the golden image;" or Peter and the apostles who said, "We ought to obey God rather than men." And we will be like Abraham who "staggered not at the promise of God through unbelief but was strong in faith giving glory to God." This is where God wants us all to be, at the point of full maturity, the maturity of Christ.

Note that Abraham, Esther, and Job were not indwelt by the Holy Spirit as we are. We have a better covenant based on better promises. We have the Helper in us, they did not! We have power from on high in us, they did not. We have spiritual authority in us, they did not. Yet, they stood courageously amid tremendous adversity and boldly and fearlessly declared their faith in God. These examples of adversity, faith, and triumph are inspiring, and challenging.

Let us remember that the children of Israel were in Egypt for four hundred years and were cruelly treated by the Egyptians. For all those years and all those generations, they moaned and groaned under their condition. Chances are that each generation cried out to God on many occasions, 'How long Lord?' or 'Why?' But nothing changed.

Even when Moses delivered God's message to Pharaoh, he became angry and things got worse for the children of Israel. It became unbearable and they were angry with Moses for making their lot harder. Sometimes when we pray, things become more difficult. Let us be aware that this is the work of the enemy to get us to doubt the promise of God and fall into unbelief. We must continue to stand our ground.

The bondage was so cruel and their sorrow so great, that God told Moses, *"I have surely seen the affliction of my people which are in Egypt and have heard their cry by reason of their taskmasters; for I know their sorrows; and I am come down to deliver them out of the hand of the Egyptians"* (Exodus 3:7,8). Note that God said to Moses, "I am come down to deliver them," even though He was sending Moses to do it. He commissioned and equipped Moses for the assignment though He was the One directing and orchestrating. See the partnership here?

This is a type of God Himself coming in the person of Jesus Christ, whom He commissioned and equipped for the assignment, to deliver us from Satan's tyranny, meanwhile directing and orchestrating everything. Remember what Jesus said? *"The Son can do nothing of himself, but what he seeth the Father do: for what things soever he doeth these also doeth the Son likewise"* (John 5:19). He also said, *"I have not spoken of myself, but the Father which sent me, he gave me a commandment, what I should say and what I should speak"* (John 12:49). And *"Believest thou not that I am in the Father and the Father in me? The words that I speak unto you I speak not of myself but the Father that dwelleth in me he doeth the works"* (John 14:10).

Hundreds of years before they ended up in Egypt God had told Abraham that his seed would be strangers afflicted in a strange land for four hundred years. Not only that, but He also told him that they would come out with abundance. After four hundred years of praying and waiting, and groaning and moaning, and waiting and praying some more, it all happened suddenly, in one day! An event that was coming for four hundred years and for many generations all happened in one day! Think about that! Many generations came and went and did not experience the deliverance that was promised. Yet it came, like clockwork, just as God said it would. God's eternal purposes will stand.

During those years and in every generation, some might have asked the question, and we can ask the question, how long? How long? Why did they have to endure four hundred years of cruelty? Why did their deliverance not come sooner? Was it because God needed some time to figure out how to deliver them? I think not! It is because, according to God's timing, it was in His predeterminate counsel that they would be afflicted four hundred years. This was already established and had to come to pass. It was also God's counsel that Moses would be the chosen one to bring their deliverance and his birth had to come at the appointed time. Therefore, it had to come to pass just the way God said because His Word is established, unchanging and unchangeable, forever settled in heaven. It may be that the processing we experience is so that the Word of God may become forever settled in our hearts and established in our lives.

Therefore, the sentence of death passed down to Adam in the Garden was not because God was angry at him for sinning, it was because His Word could not change or be changed, *"In the day that thou eatest thereof thou shall surely die"* (Genesis 2:17). God did not love Adam any less after he had sinned. God's love is never diminished because, according to Zephaniah 3:17, He rests in His love for us, meaning that His love for us never changes, He is never conflicted in His love for us, but His love requires justice, mercy, and righteousness.

CHAPTER THIRTY

All Because of Love

We are ever indebted to the One who bought us from the auction block of sin with His own precious blood. Our situation was helpless and hopeless. We were doomed and headed for eternal damnation, a dark eternity. But because of His great love for us He paid the ultimate price for our redemption. And what a price He paid for you and for me! God forbid it that we should ever take His love for granted; yet some of us are guilty of that very thing. We were born spiritually dead; hence we need to be reborn to receive eternal life, and Jesus died and rose from the dead to give us that new life.

The psalmist said, *"What shall I render unto the Lord for all of his benefits toward me? I will take the cup of salvation and call upon the name of the Lord"* (Psalm 116:13). So, all that Job experienced was for the greater good of fulfilling God's eternal purposes even as others mentioned in the Bible.

We are all part of God's tapestry in which each one of us has a special place. When we reach maturity, we're able to see things from God's perspective and we have a greater capacity to receive more of what the Father has for us. We have more of the Father's heart and want and yearn for the things that he yearns for. What grieves Him grieves us because we have His heart. This is God's desire for all of us, that we would have His heart and know His ways and His thoughts.

Again, this can only be accomplished when we abide in His Word and let His Word abide in us because without Him, we can do nothing. John 1:1 tells us, *"In the beginning was the Word, and the Word was with God, and the Word was God."* Since the Word is God, when we immerse ourselves in the Word we are immersing ourselves in God. Joshua was instructed by Moses, *"This book of the law shall not depart out of thy mouth, but thou shalt meditate therein day and night, that thou mayest observe to do according to all that is written therein, for then thou shalt make thy way prosperous, and then thou shalt have good success"* (Joshua 1:8). This is the God-given formula for success. Whatever our calling, it is the sure way to guarantee good success.

This is our Father's world. He had a plan when He made the world and created man to walk upon it and have dominion over it. Satan attempted to thwart God's plan; he was able to do this because God created Adam with a sovereign will, the will to choose. Because God knew that Adam would be deceived and be damned as a result, He made provision for his redemption. That's love! God made us for fellowship and partnership with Him and His eternal purpose for mankind was not going to be frustrated. He announced the plan of redemption in the Garden when Adam fell —Genesis 3:15. God's eternal purposes *will* stand (emphasis mine). Of course, He is the King eternal, immortal, invisible, the only wise God (1 Timothy 1:17).

God created us to be part of the wonderful plans He has for His Son, Jesus Christ, whose Body we are. Because we are part of those plans, we must endure as He endured, we share in His sufferings as we will share in His glory. We must recognize that we are not here to serve ourselves but to serve our generation with the gifts and talents He has given to us. We must recognize that we are part of a kingdom that is larger than life and look beyond ourselves to facilitate serving the needs of humanity, that is, being a blessing because we are blessed. Too many Christians think that serving others is optional. According to the scriptures we are blessed to be a blessing. As children of light, we have a responsibility, and an obligation to be the salt and the light that the world needs in our generation. *"Even as the Son of man came not to be ministered unto, but to minister, and to give his life a ransom for many"* (Matthew 20:28).

And, again, we can only accomplish this by abiding in Christ. Jesus Christ was manifested to destroy the works of the devil. He said that we, the church, would do the same works that He did and greater. I dare say that the modern church is somewhat skewed in this area, we are ever waiting to be blessed, and waiting for a blessing, waiting to be blessed and waiting for a blessing, waiting to be blessed and waiting for a blessing. Is "**being** a blessing" part of our daily routine? If not, it should be because Jesus Himself said, "I came not to be ministered unto but to minister." He also said that it is more blessed to give than to receive.

Our obligation as the church and the Body of Christ is to continue to do the works that Jesus did and greater. Since we're not doing the works we must ask ourselves why? God's Word is truth, the only truth. His Word is forever settled in heaven. It is established forever and ever. More importantly we must ask the Holy Spirit why and let Him instruct us on what to do and remain open to His instruction. We must be careful not to make excuses for this breach but ask forgiveness and seek the Holy Spirit for counsel.

I believe the answer is that we are not abiding in Christ. I believe it is because the Word of God does not have pre-eminence in our lives as it should. Other things have pre-eminence, and the Word of God is choked. Vain imaginations dominate, and the life of Christ is not evident because many refuse to die to the god of self. And the list goes on.

The Bible tells us that Job was greater in his latter end because God blessed him with twice as much as he had before, and he lived to see four generations. There is no argument that he paid a price. Like David, who came way after, Job believed to see the goodness of the Lord in the land of the living, and he was not disappointed because God is faithful.

Job was restored *after* he prayed for his friends. But he had to make the choice of obeying what God told him to do. He could have justified himself and chosen to hold a grudge because they misjudged him, but he *chose* to obey and consequently, he reaped the rewards of his obedience. Obedience is a choice.

CHAPTER THIRTY-ONE

How to Tap In

Becoming born again through faith in Jesus Christ is the door of entry into the kingdom of God, it is not the destination. Once we've entered, we must then learn of our standing in the kingdom and what is required of us as citizens of the kingdom. Then we are to learn the rules of engagement, take up arms, search out the land and take back territory, which comes in the form of winning souls for the Lord by preaching, teaching, and demonstrating the gospel of the kingdom, casting out devils and letting the oppressed go free, healing the sick, raising the dead, and preaching deliverance to the captives. Success, in this regard, is only possible if we know and obey the laws and decrees of the king, that is King Jesus.

When we enter this world, we are born into the kingdom of darkness with a rebellious nature that is hostile toward God. Hence Jesus Himself said, "Ye must be born again." When we become born again, we are now born from above with a new nature that is God-friendly, a nature that is continually reaching out toward God. With this new nature we can now discern the things of the Spirit of God: love, grace, mercy, forgiveness which are spiritually discerned.

We are here for the glory of God, the glory of the King, King of kings and Lord of lords. Our lives are not our own, but we are bought with a price, the precious blood of Jesus, the Lamb without spot or blemish. God the Father has given to us everything that we need for life and godliness and has made us partakers of His divine nature. Our spiritual position is seated with Christ in the heavenlies far above all principalities and powers, rulers, might and dominion. We have received from Christ the authority to tread upon serpents and scorpions and over all the power of the enemy. We are in Christ and Christ is in us.

When the disciples were beaten, they returned to their brethren 'rejoicing' that they were counted worthy to suffer shame for His name, the name of Jesus. They did not complain or feel sorry for themselves, but they rejoiced. Before being born again we were victims, oppressed of the devil. When we received Christ, we became victors. But to live in the reality of victors we must have our mind renewed according to the Word of God and be led by the Spirit of God. Only then can we confidently declare what the Word of God says about us, that *"we are more than conquerors through him who loved us"* (Romans 8:37).

God knows the end from the beginning, that which He says He will do He does, and that which He purposes He brings to pass for He said, *"I am God, and there is none else; I am God, and there is none like me, declaring the end from the beginning, and from ancient times the things that are not yet done, saying, My counsel shall stand, and I will do all my pleasure. I have spoken it, I will also bring it to pass; I have purposed it, I will also do it"* (Isaiah 46:10). He made us more than conquerors when He made us partakers of His divine nature through exceeding great and precious promises.

It was not a coincidence that Moses was picked up by Pharaoh's daughter. It was not a coincidence that Esther was in the right place at the right time to do the right thing even though the directive came through her uncle. And it certainly was not a coincidence that Joseph ended up as Prime Minister of Egypt.

Hence the reason that God had His Word written and preserved down through the ages. God preserved His Word so that every generation would know the truth and be made free, because according to 2 Peter 3:9, *"The Lord is not slack concerning his promise, as some count slackness; but is longsuffering to us-ward, not willing that any should perish, but that all should come to repentance."*

CHAPTER THIRTY-TWO

Don't Be Fooled

Satan, the thief, comes to steal, kill, and destroy. Jesus came to give us life and life more abundantly. Many of God's people do not experience the more than abundant life because they lack the knowledge of the Word and will of God for their lives. *"My people are destroyed for lack of knowledge"* (Hosea 4:6). Knowledge of the truth about God—that He loves us unconditionally and has provided forgive-ness of sins through His only begotten Son, Jesus Christ. About ourselves—that we are fearfully and wonderfully made in the image of God; and about each other—that we are all one in Christ, His body parts. That Christ has redeemed us from the authority of darkness and made us citizens of the kingdom of heaven.

If we arm ourselves with the truth we will not be deceived. God had His Word written and preserved down through the ages because it documents His eternal purposes concerning the earth and mankind; He created us for fellowship **and** partnership with Him, and He wanted us to know that He loves us unconditionally. He wanted to share these truths with man, His friend. Many haters of God have tried numerous times down through the ages to eradicate the Word of God from the face of the earth. Even now in our modern-day culture the haters of God are still trying to eliminate God and the Bible. But statistics show that it is still the most read book in the entire world and the most sought after. Why do you think this is?

For example, in 609 B.C Jehoiakim, king of Judah burned the scrolls written by the Prophet Jeremiah in the fire. The Roman Emperor Diocletian, in A.D. 301 to 304, burned thousands of copies of the Bible, commanded that all bibles be destroyed, and decreed that any home with a Bible in it should be burned. Rachel Barach told *Christianity Today*, "The Bible has been criticized, challenged, and banned by individuals, groups, and governments through centuries of persecution." Yet it continues to live on, relevant in every age, every generation, and every circumstance. Where are the haters of the Word of God? Where are the doubters?

Thank God He sent His Word. He sent His Word and healed us and delivered us from our distresses (Psalm 107:20). Thank God He moved men to write it (Jeremiah 30:2). *"Holy men of God spake as they were moved by the Holy Ghost"* (2 Peter 1:21). Thank God, He preserved it, *"Heaven and earth shall pass away but my word shall never pass away"* (Mark 13:31). Thank God that we have the Word of God, the absolute truth, and the absolute standard for righteousness and holiness, the source of all that is good and righteous. The Word of God is living and powerful, the Word of God is a person, the Word of God is Jesus Christ. He is the absolute standard for righteousness and holiness, the Way, the Truth, and the Life.

Job was oblivious of the discussion in heaven concerning him. He was unaware of the thief who stole his possessions, killed his children, and destroyed his life. He had limited knowledge. We know what happened because "it is written." And it was written for our learning. God did not want us to have limited knowledge concerning the issue of suffering.

CHAPTER THIRTY-THREE

Spread the Word

The Bible says that the whole world lies in wickedness. We don't have to look very far to see the death, decadence and destruction that is all around us. Without the Word of God where indeed would we be? I strongly urge you, my dear brother, my dear sister, if you haven't already done so, to make reading and becoming a doer of the living Word of the Living God a priority in your life. God wrote and preserved His Word for us so that we would not be deceived. When we neglect the Word of God, we do it to our own peril, for *"Man shall not live by bread alone but by every word that proceedeth out of the mouth of God"* (Matthew 4:4).

Then said Jesus to those Jews which believed on Him, *"If ye **continue** in my word, then are ye my disciples indeed; and ye shall know the truth, and the truth shall make you free"* (John 8:32). We must continue in the Word of God to experience the liberty of the cross.

Even though the Word of God was not yet written, yet it preserved the life of Job and countless others through troubling times; it is the same Word of God that will continue to preserve us through our journey of life. Faith comes by hearing the Word of God. Like the cloud of witnesses in the hall of faith we too will have undaunted faith because we have given the Word of God preeminence in our lives. It is the only liberator, the only temperature regulator, and the only God-positioning system for the kingdom of God. It is life itself.

Does God dwell in you? Is the Father dwelling in you? Are you allowing Him to will and do in you His good pleasure? The Bible says that it is He who works in us both to will and to do of **His** good pleasure, not your good pleasure or mine. Even Jesus said, *"I came down from heaven, not to do mine own will, but the will of Him that sent me"* (John 6:38).

Are you a yielded vessel? Have you rendered your body a living sacrifice holy and acceptable unto God? Are you dead unto sin and alive unto unrighteousness? If you are truly dead to your 'self' you are beyond offense, if you are truly dead to your 'self' you are beyond pride. I have never seen a dead man responding to an insult. I have never seen a proud dead man. I have never seen an offended dead man. Jesus bore all of these on the cross for us, our sicknesses, diseases, griefs, sorrows, rejections, and dejections. He tasted death for every man.

Job endured as seeing Him who is invisible. Moses endured as seeing Him who is invisible. The great cloud of witnesses endured as seeing Him who is invisible. Job ran with patience the race that was set before him, so did Paul and the Apostles. So have countless others down through the ages and in our present day we are enduring as seeing Him who is invisible. Because we have purposed in our heart to endure to the end we shall be saved. Because we have purposed in our heart to endure, as Job did, we will inherit the promise. *And after we have suffered a while, the Lord will make us perfect, establish, strengthen and settle us* according to 1 Peter 5:10.

Job's suffering was not in vain, and neither is ours because we judge Him faithful who promised. God trusted Job with a fiery trial knowing that He would remain faithful, knowing that His grace would be sufficient to see him through. At the end of Job's journey he was more than faithful; he now stood in awe of the Almighty, and he inherited the promise. Can God trust you with the challenge He has chosen for you? Will you thank Him for entrusting it to you even if He does not tell you why? Will you maintain your integrity as Job did? Will you remain faithful, or will you curse God and die? Will you wallow in self-pity and cloud your witness? *"But he that endures unto the end, the same shall be saved"* (Matthew 24:13*)*.

In this account of Job, as well as others mentioned, we see the value and importance of obedience. They all had to make a choice; they chose to obey God, and in every instance, it changed the course of history, for the glory of God.

They chose to obey, God was glorified, and His kingdom purposes were advanced. Likewise, when you and I choose to obey whatever God tells us to do, our obedience is rewarded, God is glorified, and His kingdom purposes are accomplished.

Is it possible that Job felt justified being angry at his fake friends who crushed his broken spirit? Who wouldn't be? Is it possible that God told Job to pray for his friends so that he could be set free from the spirit of offense and unforgiveness? Job chose to obey God, regardless of how he felt about his friends, and was set free to soar to higher heights in God. Obedience is a choice.

So, Job was restored ***after*** he prayed for his friends. It was a test of his obedience. Not for God's benefit but for Job's benefit. What would have been the result had he chosen to hold on to his anger and had not prayed for his friends? This is a lesson for those of us who are still nursing offense. This tells me that offense is a hindrance to restoration and blessing. Don't be a victim.

CHAPTER THIRTY-FOUR

What's Your Excuse?

Are you in the midst of a fiery furnace? The Lord promised to be with you when you go through the fire and you shall not be burned; He is faithful, thank Him for being with you in the fire. Are you being sifted as wheat? Let me remind you that Jesus has already prayed for you that your faith would not fail; His prayers were not limited to Peter. Do you feel like you are drowning in the flood waters of despair? Again, He promised to be with you when you pass through the waters and the rivers that they will not overflow you.

The enemy tried to destroy Job's faith, and Peter's faith, and Paul's faith, and Moses' faith, and Abraham's faith, and the faith of others. His prime target is your faith, if he can weaken or destroy your faith, he has gained territory.

Why is our faith the prime target of the enemy? Because it is the victory that overcomes the world. We overcome in Christ by our faith. It is how Job overcame, and Esther, and Abraham, and everyone else. There is a hall of faith mentioned in Hebrews Chapter 11, and we too will be inducted into that hall of faith if we keep our faith firm unto the end.

God wanted every word that He spoke to be preserved for future generations. He also wanted the efficacy of it to be preserved, so He commissioned men to write it. He oversees the maintaining and preservation of it, as when the canon was accepted by a committee of men as the official Word of God. Now we have the holy canon of scripture, the inspired written living Word of the only true and living God, the only wise God eternal, immortal and invisible.

CONCLUSION

During his earthly ministry, Jesus often asked the question, "How then shall the scriptures be fulfilled?" As the all-knowing God, Jesus never asked a question in search of an answer. This, as with all other questions, was an attempt to provoke the thoughts of His hearers. He never left them clueless, however, but provided explanations which would prepare them for their future.

Concerning our subject matter He said, "In the world you shall have tribulation but be of good cheer, I have overcome the world." Even before that, the Psalmist David told us, "Many are the afflictions of the righteous but the Lord delivers him out of them all." Later, Apostle Paul wrote, "All that will live godly in Christ Jesus shall suffer persecution."

In light of the above quoted scriptures, we must conclude that these things that were written must come to pass, that the scriptures be fulfilled.

I therefore sum up this narrative with the following scripture:

Isaiah 46:9-11

Remember the things I have done in the past. For I alone am God! I am God, and there is none like me. Only I can tell you the future before it even happens. Everything I plan will come to pass, for I do whatever I wish. I will call a swift bird of prey from the east--a leader from a distant land to come and do my bidding. I have said what I would do, and I will do it.

Thank you for reading!

www.ingramcontent.com/pod-product-compliance
Lightning Source LLC
LaVergne TN
LVHW051845080426
835512LV00018B/3077